12 Ways To Put Money In Your Pocket Every Month Without A Part-Time Job The Skinny Book That Makes Your Wallet **Fat**

Second Edition

Jennifer S. Matthews

Jean,
All the best to
you! Please stay
in touch.
Jenny

12 Ways To Put Money In Your Pocket Every Month
Without A Part-Time Job
The Skinny Book That Makes Your Wallet Fat
Second Edition

For readers of this book, individual financial results may vary. Jennifer S. Matthews, Creating Financial Literacy, LLC, and Post Foreclosure Help do not render financial, legal, tax, or real estate advice. The contents of this book are for informational purposes only. Each person reading this book is responsible for their own independent research and for obtaining professional financial, legal, tax, real estate, and any other advice sought.

The author has made every effort to provide accurate Internet addresses at the time of this publication. Neither the author nor the publisher assumes any responsibility for errors or changes that occur after publication or for third party websites or their content.

ISBN 978-0-9833864-8-3

Printed in the United States of America

This book is available at quantity discounts for bulk purchases. For information, please call 1-877-279-2701.

This book is dedicated to mom and dad for your unconditional love and support, especially during this faith walk as I do my best to humbly answer God's calling. Special thanks to Brenda Lane-Oliver, my accountability partner, sorority sister, and friend.

This book is also dedicated to everyone who reads it. My prayer is that this book helps you to breathe easier financially and take bigger steps toward making your dreams into your realities. Remember, change is good and YOU are your change!

To my friends, supporters, and prayer warriors – thank you so very much!

Table of Contents

FORWARD: How I Got Here and Why I Can Help You

With so many financial and self-help books on the market, you may be wondering which authors are legitimate and which are not. I'm guessing the title of this book caught your attention and now you're waiting to see if I deliver exactly what the title says!

I didn't luck up on the topic of personal finance or simply sit down and decide to write a book. As a matter of fact, all of this was the farthest thing from my mind! However, the first two editions of this book (one online and one in print) helped hundreds upon hundreds of people do better financially. If you take the time to sincerely and consistently apply what is covered in this book, you will do better also!

I will start the story of how I got here and why I know I can help you on Tuesday, October 31, 2000. Without looking at a calendar I know it was a Tuesday. It was the day before I was scheduled to start my new dream job. I remember a bright, sunny day that was pretty warm for that time of year because I only had on a sweatshirt and jeans.

So why are all of those details so crystal clear more than ten years later? Because that was the day I drove from Maryland to Philadelphia and was diagnosed with a very rare form of cancer in my right eye. The ten dollar name for what I had is conjunctival melanoma. Conjunctival melanoma is an extremely rare cancer of the eye, and it's known to be fatal. On November 9, 2000, I underwent successful surgery to remove the tumor.

1

Feel free to Google conjunctival melanoma along with my phenomenal surgeons Drs. Jerry and Carol Shields.

Surgery went very, very well and I kept my new job even though I only worked four days before being out five weeks for the surgery and recovery! In addition to my ongoing prayers of thanksgiving, in 2001, I started asking God to use me. I had been growing in my faith walk for several years and I wanted to show my gratitude for being healed by seeking to be used. God's answer was for me to start helping people at all income levels to improve their finances starting at a very basic level of money management.

Honestly, I laughed heartily! I thought He had bumped His Almighty and All Knowing head! I could not believe God was choosing *me* to help people with their money. Like so many of you reading this book, I never really paid much attention to the topic of money.

When I got my pay check every other week, I simply divided it into three categories: paid (i.e. outgoing money such as bills and fun money), saved, and gave (tithe). Talk about keeping it simple with the K.I.S.S. philosophy! Now God was telling (not asking!) me to wake up, step up, and be a leader to others in the area of basic money management! I was truly afraid! I was afraid of the road ahead for what He wanted me to do, and also afraid not to go ahead and do it! Remembering that my arms are too short to box with God, and that *I asked* Him to use me, I knew I had to yield and be obedient.

2

By 2002, I had started educating myself on how I could help others through my new calling. As I waded through the tons of personal finance information on the market, God was guiding and directing me. I was already an expert national trainer, and most of my experience was in the financial services industry providing software training to bankers and stock brokers.

On the formal education side, I earned a Master's degree in Professional Communication in 2001, and in 2002, I earned an MBA from The Johns Hopkins University. As for informal education, I was reading as much personal finance information as possible, and later received training as a financial coach. I also started developing workshops to deliver to organizations and businesses.

As I continued to grow my knowledge and my passion for personal finance, God was opening doors that I could not open on my own! I started attending the public meetings of The U.S. President's Council on Financial Literacy in Washington, DC. The Council was chaired by Mr. Charles Schwab. At the meetings, I met Mr. Schwab and many other great leaders in the financial education field including John Hope Bryant, Sharon Lechter, Dr. Tahira Hira, Ted Beck, Ted Daniels, and so many others!

Through those meetings and encounters, I was invited to participate in the White House Office of Faith Based and Community Initiatives Compass in Action Roundtable on

Financial Literacy in 2008; and was a Delegate at the Global Summit on Financial Literacy in 2009.

Other doors God opened included the opportunity to be a regular guest financial expert on WUSA TV9's *Mind Over Money* consumer show in Washington, DC (a CBS affiliate station) for about three years. I also participated as a subject matter expert in two PBS documentaries. The first was *Facing the Mortgage Crisis in DC*, and the second was *Pursuit of the Dream: Building Credit for Life*.

However, I too have had financial challenges. Several years ago, I left my job to pursue God's calling on my life full time. I had almost 12 months of living expenses saved and a grand plan. However, the plan was not as grand as I thought, and things definitely did not go according to my schedule.

For the first time in my life, I truly had financial problems and a whole lot of stress! One of the (many) days I prayed about my finances, God answered me with this question: "how can you expect to help people who are in financial trouble when you have never had that experience or felt that kind of pain?" And so it was!

Eighteen months after leaving my job, I accepted a temporary, contract job that on paper was not enough income to make my ends meet – but it was a job with health insurance. My financial stress continued. For two years I worked that temporary job and juggled life financially. Then, I was offered a job where I earned enough to make ends meet. I was finally able to pay down the debt I had accumulated while struggling to make ends meet in the 3½ previous years.

To stay afloat during those 3½ years and then to pay down my debt, I truly had to start using everything I had been learning about personal finance! This book contains some of the easiest things I did to have more money, and that you can do too. The information in this book alone will help you have hundreds more dollars every month if you simply (and seriously!) follow the steps!

I wanted to share my story because it is important to me that you are comfortable with who is providing you with information, their source(s), and their motives. I, with a little "i" am providing you with information that is guided by Him with a capital "H" as the Source. I don't have any motives. I did not choose to do this, I was chosen. I believe I must do my best to serve God and carry out His will with excellence. My idea of serving with excellence means providing quality information and resources that can lead to many great opportunities for you and your future!

My story of how I got here and who is guiding me is exactly why I know I can help you and anyone else who sincerely wants to change their financial future. Readers of this book typically create $300 - $500 per month from within their current income, with one reader creating over $1,000 each month!

My focus and goal are to provide you with simple, immediate steps you can take to have more money for the things you want to do. For example, do you want to buy a house? Use this book to help you raise your credit scores and create cash for your down payment. Do you want to save for retirement and/or your children's tuition? Use this book to help you have cash available to open investment accounts with a financial planner. Whatever your desire is that you need cash for, you can follow the simple steps in this book to get the cash you need. Keep reading as I share information you can take immediate action on to move yourself closer and closer to your goals and dreams!

I encourage you to open your heart and your mind to the information and ideas contained on the pages of this book. Also, I encourage you to honor yourself by taking all of the time that is necessary to complete each action step in each chapter with excellence!

Words from People Who Already Read this Book...

I purchased this book at my church. I only bought it to support Jennifer on her journey to help others become financially stable. I never imagined that several months later I would have to use some of her money saving tips!

I became unemployed and my family was now living off of my husband's one income. It started to become overwhelming. We had more bills than money! I remembered reading Jennifer's book and what it said about re-evaluating and cutting down on monthly bills. I started reading it a second time and this time I followed the steps...

- *I called my cable company and was able to negotiate a package that is more affordable for us. I was able to reduce my cable bill by $50 a month, just by removing a few channels we weren't using.*

- *I called my mobile carrier and was able to negotiate a package with them. By the time I was done, I saved $100 a month on my cell phone bill! I learned that cell phone carriers are always willing to work something out with you, before they lose your business. Not only did I reduce my bill by $100, I'm also entitled to one additional free line if I ever need it.*

- *My husband was buying his breakfast and lunch every day, spending about $12-$15 a day. Now he takes his breakfast and lunch to work. This not only ended up saving us anywhere from $240-$300 every month, but he now eats healthier too!*

This adds up to $390-$450 every month! The best part is, after doing all of this and realizing how much we are saving, we now look for other ways to save! We have not solved all of our money problems, but the information in this book has definitely made a huge difference in our finances and has made it a lot easier for us!

I recommend this book to everyone! Even if you aren't struggling with your finances, you just never know what your future holds. Plus, who doesn't want to save money?

Thanks Jennifer! Your book really opened up our eyes to a brand new world of saving money!
-Deborah Barnes

I loved your book! It's short and to the point, which is great because I'm not an avid reader. Everything in the book makes sense! Finally a book that actually does what it says it's going to do!
-Toni Jones

In 2008, Jennifer shared some of the principles in her book with me. I didn't think I could save $400 every month, but with Jennifer's help, I've actually been saving more than that ever since!
-J. Reid

In April, 2011, I was in such financial turmoil that I couldn't see the light of day. I turned to my church. My Pastor gave me a copy of 12 Ways to Put Money in Your Pocket Every Month Without A Part Time Job, and asked Ms. Matthews to provide me with financial counseling. The first thing she told me to do was to be honest about my debt and to figure out my monthly expenses. To do this, she made me write out my budget, and then adjust my spending habits so I could get back on track. Reading this book made making these adjustments very easy! Using what I learned in this book and my own self-determination, I was back on track after just two months of strict budgeting and watching my money. Four months later, I was able to fly away for a beach vacation with my friends. I was on a budget while there, but still had a really fun time! Thanks to Ms. Matthews' book, I am now paying all of my bills on time and am also able to save $150 every month while going to school to finish my graduate degree.

Que Campbell

Introduction

12 Ways To Put Money In Your Pocket Every Month Without A Part-Time Job. Is this title fact or fiction? Well, in a few short pages, you will surely find out! Why are you reading this book?

A. Working a part-time job and want to quit
B. Need to have more cash available every month
C. Laid off or do not have job security
D. Curious
E. Don't believe the title, so reading to prove yourself correct
F. Other

Be honest with yourself. If your answer is A through D then most likely, you have some financial questions or challenges that you may or may not understand, or may not be willing to face. According to articles in Forbes™ magazine and The Huffington Post™, Warren Buffet, one of the United States' wealthiest people, admitted to making financial mistakes and to having financial concerns soon after the first recession started. If Mr. Buffet can be that open and honest, the rest of us need to confess too!

Even if you still have your income, declining property values and decreases in retirement and college savings funds have created challenges and/or concerns for many. For the millions who lost their job or experienced decreases in income such as reduced work hours or furlough days, the challenges and concerns are even greater.

9

Many people do not really understand money, nor do they know the right financial questions to ask because the subject is not taught in most homes or schools. So to make up for this lack of understanding, many people cover the problem with part-time jobs; or they keep pretending that things are OK; or they believe that things are going to get better on their own. Another big outcome of this lack of understanding is a lack of good, consistent money management skills and habits. However, the changes in the economy are forcing people to pay close attention to their finances and to consider new ideas and options - and that's great!

It is very important to accept that you probably have some financial challenges, and then COMMIT TO YOURSELF that you are going to *consistently take massive and immediate action* to solve your financial challenges so you can begin to breathe easier and eventually no longer be part of the financially struggling population! For most people, this means regularly spending time working on tasks you don't like or don't want to do. However, the pay-off is huge! Accept the fact that you did not get into your current financial condition overnight, and therefore know that you will not get out of it overnight. Additionally, understand that you will have to work hard at turning your money around – but you can make it happen!

Consistently using all of the information in this book every month for one year will create new spending habits, new ways to manage money, and a bank account that proves your success!

This will be the result of the commitment you just made to yourself to consistently take massive and immediate action on your finances.

Let's put this another way... Think about your past vacations, family reunions, celebrations, or other major occasions you planned. Let's pretend that you are planning another one six months from now, and we'll use an island vacation in our example. What are the steps you need to take to make this island vacation fabulous? Some of the steps are: choosing an island, getting airfare, selecting a hotel, getting your passport, and looking for fun things to do while you are there. As the date gets closer, you start thinking about what you will wear, what you need to buy before you get there, spending money, and so much more!

Hopefully this trip planning example made your mind wander to a beautiful, far off exotic place! Now as we snap back to reality, how is it that most of us have no problem spending months planning vacations, retirement parties, family reunions, and other special occasions, but we don't take nearly the same amount of time planning how we spend the paycheck we get every other week (or however often you are paid)? It's this regularly scheduled income that sustains our existence in life; however, we don't consistently plan for how we will spend it! This is exactly what a spending plan (or budget) does for us and why we all must have one!

11

A spending plan is a written plan for how we spend our paychecks and other sources of income. An ongoing spending plan is just like planning a vacation or other special occasion. The more you plan for your vacation, party, or other occasion, the less stress and more fun you usually have! Similarly, the more you use an ongoing spending plan, the more fun and less stress you can have in life because you will have more money that will hopefully be put to the best uses. Get a spending plan template on the Free Downloads page on my website at www.CreatingFinancialLiteracyLLC.com

According to Kim Khan in an article for MSN's Money Central, 43% of Americans spend more than they earn.[1] This means people making $25,000 a year often spend far more, say $30,000 and up! People making $100,000 a year, often spend over $120,000. So, it doesn't matter how much money you make, because when you spend more than you make *you* will create financial challenges! This spending statistic was reported prior to the collapse of the housing and financial markets. With so many people ending up with mortgages they could not afford, the numbers of people spending more than they earn has actually gone up. People who rent their home or apartment are also often spending more than they earn in this economy.

Without a spending plan and a self-commitment to improving our finances, it is very easy to get used to the habit of

---

[1] Khan, Kim. How Does Your Debt Compare.
http://moneycentral.msn.com/content/SavingandDebt/P70741.asp

spending more than we make because buying for ourselves and others makes us feel good in a world that can sometimes make us feel not so good. However, when income goes down or even goes away, or a critical unexpected expense pops up, it hits us harder because we are already spending more than we make, which means the money gap that needs to be closed is larger. You may be surprised to know how many people have combined balances that are less than $200 in their primary checking and savings accounts on the day before payday - even prior to the country's economic downturn!

To make it more difficult for us to spend less, the financial industry, the media, and society are constantly bombarding us with messages that encourage us to spend, Spend, SPEND! Everyday we're constantly and repeatedly inundated with ads for things to make us happier, skinnier, fatter, more popular, more relaxed, lazier, sexier, prettier, and more. Then the financial industry tells us that for everything else we want, we can pay for it with a credit card!

Advertising is everywhere! The constant repetition of these messages helps keep many people in spending cycles that make it hard to address our financial challenges. These various industries want all of us to stay in spending cycles that benefit *them* financially instead of benefiting *our* wallets. These industries don't want you to stick with the 12 simple ways to create money explained in this book. They don't want you to start creating cash to resolve your financial challenges!

13

Financial challenges can come from spending more than is being earned; decreases in income; mortgage and real estate issues; carrying balances on credit cards every month that you can't pay off; unexpected expenses; and more. At the start of the recession, the statistics on the numbers of households carrying at least one credit card with a balance every month ranged from high to staggering, depending upon the source.

Here are few questions to answer. If you answer 'yes' to any one question, this book can help!

- Have you ever had a heated discussion with your spouse or significant other over money?
- Have you used Caller ID to screen bill collectors?
- Did you ever not go out with friends because you didn't have the money?
- Have you ever denied your child something they really wanted because of money?

You are not alone if you answered 'yes' to any of these questions. However, if you take massive and immediate action on what you are about to read, you will change these answers in the future!

Creating Money with Money Opportunities

This book shares 12 simple ways to create a minimum of $240 in extra money every month by looking at 12 expenses most people have, and then showing how to adjust each expense by a minimum of $20. That is a minimum of $240 back in your pocket every month, which is almost $3,000 every year!

However, most people who read earlier versions of this book actually created much more than $240 every month! If that's enough to make you breathe easier financially then you may not need to get a part-time job! To create *your* money, you have to be very honest with yourself and you have to commit to sticking with each of these 12 steps each and every month.

Each of these 12 expenses is an opportunity for you to create money, so we call them Money Opportunities. Years ago one of my financial mentors taught me a principle that I have come to live by: *Money is only an idea. People who lack money simply lack ideas.* The 12 Money Opportunities in this book are ideas that when used consistently will create money for you each and every month!

Each Money Opportunity is very simple, although how easy it is to for you to create money with them depends on how committed you are to changing your financial picture. But guess what… if you are serious and truly committed to changing your finances, you will see that some of the Money Opportunities will create much more than $20! This will give you the opportunity for even more cash every month, meaning more money in your pocket! And, you're not going to have to become a hermit, or drastically change your life or your lifestyle! If anything, you will improve your lifestyle!

This book is interactive, so grab a pen or pencil so you can write on the pages. Each of the 12 Money Opportunities ends with you going to the back of the book to write down how much cash you created from that Opportunity. To help you create more money with the Money Opportunities, you need to focus on "why" you are going to take the time read this book and seriously apply what you read. Writing your reasons "why" you are going to make these changes *now* is very important! As human beings, we are visual and we achieve our goals better when they are in writing and placed where we can see them every day.

Writing down your thoughts, goals, and spending is a very powerful requirement for your success. Start here by jotting down your thoughts on what you have read so far. How do you see yourself financially today? Why do you see a need to change what you have been doing financially in the past?

_____

_____

_____

Next, list 3 practical things you will do with the money you are about to create that will _help_ your financial situation. Know that if you create $300 every month using this book and you use $200 to pay down debt and spend $150, that's $350 and you will be worse off than before you read the book!

1._____

_____

2._____

_____

3._____

_____

Understand that even though the book title includes the phrase "without a part-time job"; I am a firm believer in multiple streams of income. Your extra income can come from a part-time job, a home-based business, real estate investing, and other sources. What is critically important with your primary income, as well as your other income streams, is proper money management so that the extra income is available to go toward your goals and dreams. For your extra income to make a difference, you have to be able to *see* that difference!

Here is a visual example of what I mean by proper money management and seeing the difference. Picture a big pot of red spaghetti sauce simmering on the stove. You get some nice green herbs, such as basil and oregano, and sprinkle them on top. You stir the pot and the herbs disappear! Yummy? ...that depends! If your primary income source is like the pot of spaghetti, and you are not managing it as well as you should or could, what happens when you add more income to the pot? ...it disappears just like the basil and oregano! When the main sources of money in your life are not properly managed and you add more money to it, that money disappears in the "pot" of mismanagement! So, while you are working part-time and/or are generating income from other sources, make sure you take the time to take control over the management of all of your money so that you can *see* the difference your extra time and efforts outside of your primary income source are making!

So many people feel like their walls are closing in around them. If you feel like your financial walls are closing in around you, then get out of your box! You can do it and this book is written in a way that will guide you!

Now it's time to make *your* wallet fat with *your* 12 Money Opportunities!

Money Opportunity #1
Home Telephone Bill

Before going through each Money Opportunity, you must understand the true difference between a need and a want. A need is an essential, minimum requirement that is truly required for us to live. Everything beyond our true minimum requirements is something that we want, something we enjoy the convenience of, and/or something we enjoy the "status" or appearance of having.

Simple examples include being hungry and needing food vs. going to a pricey restaurant and ordering the most expensive thing on the menu. Another example is that many of us need a car because of the limited amount of public transportation available where we live. However, there is a difference between a safe, fuel efficient car with a $350 monthly payment and a luxury car with a big gas tank and a $700 monthly payment. Both cars will get you safely from point A to point B, except one will have you arrive with more money in your pocket.

Both of these examples meet our need for food and transportation; however, they leave very different amounts of money in our wallet at the end of every month! As you go through each of these Money Opportunities, take the time to take a good, hard look at what each expense is costing you. If you find it hard to make the changes, go back and look at what you wrote about *why* you are committed to making changes in your financial life and what you will do with the money created once you start seeing it every month.

Get your home telephone bill out and read it line-by-line and page-by-page, including all of the fine print. After you have finished, read it a second time! You may unknowingly be paying for services you did not ask for or do not need. As you read your bill over and over again, line-by-line, look at the cost for services you do not *absolutely* need, such as:

Feature Needed?	Yes	No	Amount Saved
Call waiting			
Call forwarding			
3-way calling			
Caller ID			
Maintenance plans			
Other features that cost money			

Questions to ask and research:
- If your cell phone has some or all of these features, then do you need to pay for them on your home phone too?
- Do you really need unlimited long distance on your home phone or is basic service all you truly need?
- Is it less expensive to have unlimited long distance on your home phone and lower your minutes plan on your cell phone? Or, drop long distance at home and have a cell phone plan with unlimited minutes?
- Ask your telephone service provider about package discounts including bundling long distance, internet, and cell phone services for discounts.

- What are competitor telephone companies offering for the home telephone service features you truly need?
- Some cable companies now offer telephone and internet service; and some telephone companies offer television and internet services. How do their prices, discounts, and bundled services compare?

Go to the Money Opportunity Log at the end of this book and write in the amount of money created by researching options that will lower your home telephone bill. The goal is to create at least $20 from each Money Opportunity. Were you able to lower your telephone bill by $20? Great! If not, review your bill in detail again. Don't be discouraged if you still do not create $20. Remember that some Money Opportunities will put far more than $20 a month in your pocket, so the average will likely work out for you.

This is your first Money Opportunity. You may not have realized that each Opportunity will make you think hard, do some research, and then take action to make the adjustment! If your boss said I'll give you an extra $3,000 every year if you make adjustments to these 12 line items, you would do it without thinking twice about it! Well, you are the boss of your life, and this book has 12 Money Opportunities for you to adjust to give yourself $3,000 or more! If you talked yourself out of putting forth the energy and effort needed to do the research to make your phone bill adjustments, be your own boss and tell yourself to go back and start over! ...remember there's $3,000 or more in it for you! Also remember that each Money Opportunity is simple, but the ease in which you can create money with each opportunity totally depends on you!

IMPORTANT NOTE: I believe it is very important to have a home phone/land line, especially in homes with children, senior citizens, or anyone with serious health issues. In the event of an emergency, home phones will usually automatically display the address to the emergency dispatcher. This is extremely helpful if the caller is nervous and/or if the caller is injured and cannot speak. Another advantage is that home phones are usually kept in the same place and can be located much faster in an emergency than a cell phone, which may be anywhere in the home, including inside of purses, pockets, and bags.

Money Opportunity #2
Cell Phone Bill

This is probably a touchier subject than the home phone bill because so many people are convinced by friends, the media, and advertisers into thinking they *need* their cell phones more than they actually do! Many people think they *need* a fancier, prettier, more cool, more expensive, and smarter phone when the truth is they really only *want* these features in spite of the expenses that come with them. When it comes to cell phones and features, too many people are paying lots of money for what they want instead of their actual basic cell phone needs!

Before you start reading your cell phone bill, you need to decide if you want to work a part-time job and/or continue to be financially challenged just because:

- My cell phone looks cool or makes me look/feel important
- I want my email now at a cost of $$$ per year instead of waiting until I get home to check my email (multiply the cost of your data plan by 12 months and look at the cost difference between your cell phone and one that is not data enabled)
- My bill is high because of the features and "stuff" on my bill that goes far beyond my true basic cell phone needs
- My bill is high because my (unemployed) kids have costly phone features they want for popularity instead of what is truly needed to reach someone in case of an emergency
- I'm paying the cell phone bill for my adult child(ren) who should find a way to pay their own bill

Right about now your inner voice is probably working overtime trying to convince you that you really do need your particular type of cell phone and all the features, especially the PDAs, smart phones, and music phones! Plus your mind also may be telling you that you should have never started reading this book because the author doesn't understand chic, cool, prestige, or about being part of the "in" crowd!

My advice to you: forget the 'in' crowd because living like them will not help you change your financial situation. When you reach the point that you are so focused on your goals that you are willing to make financial changes regardless of what others think, or what you see and hear in the media, your financial situation will change by leaps and bounds!

Remember, the steps in this book are simple but how easy they are to implement depends upon how attached you are to material things. Is it more important to have money in your pocket and your bank account, or only look like you might – when the real truth is you may be dead broke and struggling financially?

My personal definition of 'dead broke' is someone working full-time who has less than $200 easily accessible in a checking or savings account on the day before payday. I admit that at more than one time in my life, I have been dead broke by my own definition! Also, if you have to pay a fee or penalty to access your $200, such as a CD, IRA, 401K, holiday club account, etc., then that money does not count.

However, I firmly believe that you should have money stashed away that is making money for you in multiple savings vehicles such as those just mentioned and others. You should consult a financial planning expert and then research their recommendations to determine which savings vehicles are right for your current financial situation and your financial goals. After reading this book and consistently acting on the information in it, you will have extra money every month to put away into various types of savings and investment accounts, and into investments that generate income.

The point I am making with the availability of $200 on the day before payday is that most people struggle to make it from one paycheck to the next. Having an additional $240, $300, or $500 every month, (as this book is showing you how to create) will make a major financial difference for many readers. For some readers, the amount created may even be all you need to keep from being evicted or foreclosed upon. And yes, it is very true that the unemployment rate and mortgage crisis have created some exceptional challenges in many households. These challenges make it hard, and even impossible, for these families to have $200 available. However, do not continue to be a victim of this economy! Keep reading and do what it takes to set yourself up for victory!

Now that we've had another reminder of why we have to apply the information in this book, let's get back to the cell phone bill. Do exactly what you did with your home phone bill for your cell phone bill. Get your cell phone bill out and read it line-by-line, including the fine print. After you have finished, read it a second time! Once again, you may unknowingly be paying for services you did not ask for or do not need.

As you read your bill over and over again, line-by-line, look for services you don't *absolutely* have to have. Here are some examples to research:

Feature Needed?	Yes	No	Amount Saved
Call waiting			
Call forwarding			
3-way calling			
Data plans			
Family plans			
Excess minutes and texting			
Ring tones			
Music downloads			
Text messaging			
Upgraded phones and phone features			
Camera and picture downloading			
Maintenance plans			
Other features that cost money			

Questions to ask and research:

- How many cell phone minutes do you use each month? Do you need all of the minutes you are paying for? What other plans does your carrier offer?

- Can you use a landline that has flat rate billing to make most phone calls instead of a pay per use or minutes per use cell phone? This may allow you to reduce your cell phone minutes plan, thus lowering your bill.

- Is it less expensive to have unlimited long distance on your home phone and lower your minutes plan on your cell phone or vice versa?

- What are competitor cell phone companies offering for the cell phone features you truly need? If the savings over the next few months are more than the cost of the early termination fee, then it may be worth it to pay the early termination fee. Crunch the numbers on a calculator so you can make an informed decision!

- Check with your employer, school, and organizations you belong to and ask if they have relationships that provide discounts with certain cell phone providers.

- If you get other services from your cell phone provider, such as home telephone service, ask if they offer a discount to have all the charges combined into one bill.

- For children's cell phones, ask your cell phone company about plans that only allow users to dial certain numbers. For example, for half of what you pay now, perhaps your child's cell phone can be programmed to only dial home, your office, grandparents, and one or two other emergency contact numbers. This eliminates them running up charges talking to friends and text-messaging that *you* feel you have to pay for! These plans also work great for college students. Get them a dorm phone landline for local calls with no long distance and a cell phone that dials specific long distance numbers. Or, they can get a job and pay for their own cell phone with a bill that is in their name! By the way, aren't children supposed to be focused on school and school work instead of talking and texting?

- The next time you or a family member needs a new cell phone – *only* because the current one is broken – make certain you purchase a phone model you can pay cash for without impacting that month's household bills and savings!

Also know that most "free" upgrades such as phones, features, and services offered by cell phone companies are simply marketing tactics to lock you into a new, extended service contract! Choose your upgrades carefully. Make sure you ask lots of questions. When your questions are answered, hang up and take time to check with competitor companies. Don't be fooled or pressured by "gotta buy it today" specials!

Go to the Money Opportunity Log at the end of this book and write in the amount of money created from reviewing your cell phone bill. Were you able to lower your bill by at least $20? Great! ...After just two Money Opportunities you are already putting up to $40 or more into your pocket every month!

Money Opportunity #3
Lunch and Snacks at Work

This is a biggie! How often do you eat out? In the morning, do you grab a cup of gourmet coffee or a donut? Or, do you stop at the convenience store or drive through a fast food eatery each morning? Do you grab a sandwich at lunch? Do you make a mid-afternoon trip to the vending machine for an energy boost or to satisfy a sweet tooth craving? And, after a hard day at work, do you end the day by picking up something on the way home because you don't feel like cooking or you have to go to a meeting or pick the kids up?

How many of these scenarios fit you each day, each week, or each month? Do you realize that the $4 breakfast; $8 lunch; $1 afternoon snack; and $10 dinner add up to $23 per day! With 20 workdays in a month, this totals a whopping $460 per month! Even if you don't do each of these every day, the breakfast alone is $80 a month!

If what you just read made you grunt or groan, plan to create at least $50 per month from this Money Opportunity alone. If what you read made you feel uneasy or you broke out into a sweat, then you need to convert a full 50% of your restaurant food spending into cash that stays in your pocket every month!

If you eat lunch out, buy breakfast, or buy snacks daily or even regularly, you will be amazed at how much money you will save by making a few simple adjustments! There are ways to still

29

enjoy some of your daily conveniences while enjoying the savings:

- Take your lunch to work at least two or three days every week:
    o Take sandwiches and/or salads because they are quick and easy!
    o Take a frozen dinner that was on sale in the grocery store. These quick, hot meals can cost as little as $2 each on sale! You can keep salt, pepper, and other favorite spices in your desk drawer to add a little more flavor (Note: Be mindful of the sodium content in some frozen meals)
- Cook two large meals on the weekend. Use one for lunch during the week and the other for dinner. This will save you money and keep you from eating the same thing for both lunch and dinner.
- Buy bottled water, soda, and your favorite snack items when on sale in the grocery store. Keep them in or under your desk at work, or bring them in daily. This will keep your afternoon snack costs way down.
- Keep a case of bottled water in the trunk of your car. This is great for anytime you or your passengers get thirsty while you're on the go, and it also provides liquid refreshment after a gym workout. Keep the water in a cooler in the trunk in warm weather, and add reusable ice packs every few days to keep the water cool.
- Purchase coffee beans from your favorite coffee shop. Put a lamp timer on your kitchen coffee pot and set it so that a fresh pot of your favorite brand of coffee is ready to go every morning when you are leaving home. Experiment with different creamers, flavorings, etc. and see if you can come up with your own new favorite gourmet flavor! This will keep you from buying coffee on your way to work. Depending upon your employer,

you may be able to place a small coffee maker on your desk and have the same treat at work.

- If you achieve a major goal or accomplishment, treat yourself to your favorite latte or snack once a month. However, make certain that your earned treat does not send you back into your old spending habits, which could mean back to having financial challenges!

Think about your part-time job, your ongoing financial struggles, and any stress that comes from them. What difference would adjustments of $50, $100, or $200 every month in this Money Opportunity make in your life? Realize that a $200 adjustment is $50 each week or just $10 each day! If you are serious about taking control over your money and ending your financial challenges, then you will be willing to stretch yourself to make some tough adjustments in this category. **Understand that this Money Opportunity must be diligently revisited every month.** You may need to revisit this category each week to make sure you stay on target!

Remember this eating out expense applies to your spouse and children too! How much money do you give your children each day for lunch and junk food? Is this on top of their allowance? They can take their lunch a few days each week. Children need to understand their role ***and responsibility*** in the family's finances!

Yes, children need to understand money and spending at a level that's age-appropriate for them. If a child can ask you to buy them something, then certainly they are old enough to be taught about needs vs. wants, spending, and how money works!

Share your knowledge and experiences with them. Let them help with the Money Opportunity adjustments. Log on to *www.CreatingFinancialLiteracyLLC.com* and click on the Free Downloads page for a list of youth financial education resources. Also on the website are numerous games you and your children can play. There are games for all ages, from toddlers through seniors!

Go to the Money Opportunity Log at the end of this book and write the amount created by adjusting your eating out expenses, especially during the workweek. Were you able to find ways to create at least $100 in this Money Opportunity? That's only $25 per week, which is simply $5 per workday!

Some readers have already created more than $200 cash to put in their pocket every month ($2,400 per year!) and we've only covered three Money Opportunities! *WOW!!!* How does the money you've discovered so far make you feel? I hope your answer is somewhere between great and terrific!

Money Opportunity #4
Utility Bills

Depending upon where you live, your electric and gas utility bills may be separate or combined. For this Money Opportunity, you will need all bills related to your gas, electric, and water utility expenses.

It goes without saying that you want to turn all the lights off in rooms that are not occupied. If you have small children, make a game out of having them catch someone leaving a light on in an empty room. You may decide that whoever they catch has to give them $.25 up to $1 for them to put in their piggy bank each time they are caught. If you have older children, deduct $1 out of their allowance or other money for every light they leave on. You can put this money aside and use it for a family pizza and movie night when the total gets large enough.

In addition to turning lights off, replace your current light bulbs with compact fluorescent bulbs. These bulbs cost a little more than standard light bulbs, however they use 75% less electricity and last up to ten times longer than standard light bulbs.

Know that there are numerous "silent" energy draws in your home. Everything plugged into an outlet *always* draws power. Even though microwaves, computers, printers, big screen TVs are all turned off, they actually *always* draw power, which can cost you lots of money! As an example, think about your microwave. You may use it a total of 15 minutes each day to

33

heat up a few things here and there. However, since it's plugged in for 24 hours, you're paying the electric bill for the 23 hours and 45 minutes that it's not actually being used!

To stop this silent energy waster, you can keep these items unplugged or plug them into a power strip and turn the power strip off. Turning the power strip off stops the silent energy draw. However, if you plug your computer into a power strip, make sure you still plug the strip into a surge protector. Turn the power strip off, but leave the surge protector turned on and plugged directly into the wall. Also, always leave your refrigerator and washing machine plugged in.

Another way to reduce electric and gas expenses is to eat salad and other raw foods for dinner two nights per month so the stove does not get turned on. You will save money and eat healthy at the same time! Use leftover baked fish and chicken to go on top of salads and for tacos because these meats can be eaten cold. There are lots of great ways to satisfy your stomach without using the stove...be creative! If you're not the creative cook, get ideas from books and magazines at your local library and from websites.

Turning the thermostat down 3 to 5 degrees in the winter and up 3 to 5 degrees in the summer is another money saver. This change in your thermostat setting by a just a few degrees will lower your utility bill. If there are seniors or very small children in your home, make sure they do not get chilled or too warm with the adjusted air temperatures. I personally used all of these tips to cut my November 2008 electric bill in half! This simple adjustment really can make a difference.

If your house is heated with oil, fill your oil tank in the spring or at the start of the summer. Home heating oil prices are usually lower then because there is less demand. This will lower your average oil bill for the season.

Here is the electric bill savings tip that may challenge some of you the most, but will definitely give you the maximum benefit in multiple ways! ...Keep the TV turned off and unplugged one extra hour every day to read a financially empowering book or magazine. Have your children read a book on a topic of interest to them at the same time!

You are reading this book because you have some concerns about your finances that may range from mild to serious. However, if you are like most people, you spend more time entertaining yourself than you do educating yourself with information that can change your financial future and your life in general. Not educating yourself with empowering information is a sure way to prolong the amount of time you feel the stress and strain from financial and other challenges!

By watching negative and/or non-empowering television shows, and all the media advertising on TV, you are not growing yourself or learning productive ways to address and eventually end your financial challenges. Instead, you are spending money on electricity, and probably cable too, to fill your mind with information that is often negative, as well as more ways and ideas to spend money you don't have! We often call this relaxing, unwinding, or (truly) mindless TV. Even the 44th President of the United States called for everyone to read more! Don't let reading become a lost art in your home!

If you leave the television off one additional hour every day, including weekends, you will cut approximately 30 hours of usage from your electric bill every month! You probably pay taxes to have a free library in your community. Put your tax dollars to work, get a library card, and start reading some of the books on the list at the back of this book.

Take your children to the library with you and make reading an everyday family activity. Reading library books is a great way to expand the imaginations of smaller children and help older children explore interests that may help them choose a career or entrepreneurial path.

Another way to save on both gas and electric bills is to check each window and door that leads to the outside of your home for drafts. If there is a draft, your energy dollars are being wasted! Checking for wasteful drafts is easy and takes less than ten minutes! Grab some toilet paper, about three sheets in length, and hold it along the top, bottom, sides, and center of every window and door. If the tissue moves when you are holding it still, there is a draft and your money is being wasted.

To seal the draft go to your local home or hardware store and explain your findings to the clerk. The clerk can recommend solutions to fix the problem, which will save you money.

Perform this check in newer homes too because they settle into the ground and doors and windows may no longer fit tightly.

To create money with your water bill, you can make a few inexpensive changes at home. Change all of your shower heads to water-saving models. This change will allow you to use less water, which also cuts the cost of heating the water because there is less being used. Make certain none of your plumbing is leaking. If you are not sure, let the water run for one minute in every sink and tub in your home (one at a time). Turn the water off, and then take a tissue or toilet paper and wipe each plumbing valve and connection, including the pipes under the sinks. If there is any moisture on the tissue, you may have a leak. For your toilets, place a tissue or napkin around the base. Leave it there for a day or two (long enough for the toilet to be used several times) and see if it shows signs of wetness.

Other ways to save on the water bill include taking a bath instead of a long shower, or taking a short shower instead of a long one. When using the dishwasher or washing machine, make certain you only wash full loads and use cool water temperature settings when possible.

Go to the Money Opportunity Log at the end of this book and write the amount saved on your utility bills that will now be in your pocket. This savings will probably change each month, especially if you live in an area that experiences extreme changes in climate. For this Money Opportunity the goal is to create an average monthly savings that is a minimum of $20. If you receive one bill for electricity and a separate bill for gas, you should work to save $20 on each bill for an average total of $40 per month. Since water bills are usually not too expensive, you may only save an average of $5 - $10 each month or each quarter.

Money Opportunity #5
Carpools and Errands

Make a conscious effort to consolidate errands. Often errands can be grouped together into one trip. If your town is large, plan ahead so you can take care of all your needs on a particular side of town in the same trip.

Another great savings is to carpool and keep your car parked a minimum of two days each month. With a little planning, you can probably carpool to work and to your children's extra curricular activities. Share rides with other parents who are looking to save money too.

If public transportation is available, use it to get to work a few days each month. This creates additional quiet time for reading, meditation, and other things that the hustle and bustle of a busy life may not allow you to do as often as you like or need to.

Take a moment to calculate the cost of gas, tolls, and parking for your work commute. Public transportation and carpooling may be a greater savings than it appears to be! Also think of alternative forms of transportation including bicycles, walking, and scooters.

Go to the Money Opportunity Log at the end of this book and write in the amount saved on errands and carpooling expenses. This may be a little difficult to calculate because every tank of gas costs a different amount, but it's important to try anyway.

39

For example, if you currently buy gas 4 times each month, but only bought gas 3 times because of this Money Opportunity, then record the average cost of one tank of gas as your savings. Another example is if you paid $100 per month to park at work and purchased a one month transportation pass for $80 instead, then you would record the $20 difference plus the average cost of the one tank of gas saved! Were you able to put at least $20 in your pocket from adjustments in this Money Opportunity? Great!

Money Opportunity #6
Increasing Credit Scores

This is a major expense that people overlook, mostly because they don't understand credit scores or don't know how to fix low credit scores. Credit scores are even more important during the current condition of the US economy. If you truly want to change your financial picture, you must know and monitor your credit scores! If any two of your credit scores are less than 680, then your scores are probably costing you money! The lower your credit scores, the more you pay in interest on credit cards, borrowed money, insurance (car, life, etc.), and other important items.

There are three widely recognized credit reporting agencies, TransUnion, Equifax, and Experian (formerly TRW), and each of your credit reports and scores may be different. If you have not checked your credit reports within the last six months, you need to! You can get one free copy of each of your three credit reports every year from *www.annualcreditreport.com*. These free reports do not include your credit score; however, they will allow you to monitor your credit reports for errors and items that need to be improved upon or disputed.

If you do not know your credit score, go to *www.myfico.com* and purchase one credit report and your FICO score. At this point you may only need to pay for one FICO score from one of the three credit reporting agencies, preferably Equifax because more creditors report to them. This critical information costs about $15. Right now there's no real need to purchase the other offerings on the FICO website; however, I strongly recommend taking the time to read the information on the website and educating yourself about what goes into your credit scores.

Many major companies use credit scores to help them determine how risky it is to do business with you -- meaning loaning you money, giving you credit, etc. Credit scores are used to determine car insurance rates; credit card interest rates; loan approvals and interest rates; apartment security deposit amounts; mortgages; and much, much more! Employers often check credit scores as part of the pre-employment process, and may withdraw employment offers to candidates with low credit scores! Losing a job offer because of credit scores is not something anyone can afford, especially in this economy!

Remember, it's important to keep your credit score higher than 680, and preferably over 740! If your credit scores are under 700, take steps to repair your credit or have it repaired by a reputable company *after* you have verified their independent references. Understand that 35% of your credit score is based upon paying your bills on time and 30% is based upon keeping credit card balances low. This means, we control 65% of our credit scores!

If you have lots of debt and you are considering debt consolidation and/or debt management plans (DMP), it is important to know that these programs will more than likely lower your credit scores, regardless of what the sales agent tells you. There are ways to get out of debt without debt settlement, debt management, and even bankruptcy.

Finally, do not pay up front fees for credit repair or any debt plans. It is illegal under Federal law for credit repair companies to charge a fee before the credit repair services are completed! Be certain to read any contracts fully and carefully. Before you sign anything with any agency, ask for a copy of all contracts and documents to take with you. Go home, read them, give them to someone else to read, and only sign and return the documents after you are *absolutely certain* the company is legitimate *and* that you fully understand everything in the documents. If the agency will not give you copies of the paperwork to take home prior to signing them, refuse to do business with that company!

There are many scam companies out there preying on the emotions and the critical financial situations some people are in. It is important to make sure you verify any credit repair and/or debt companies with the Attorney General's Office in your state and in the state(s) where the business is both incorporated and headquartered. This may mean three different states: where you live, where the company is headquartered, and where the company is incorporated. Some non-profit organizations are fake and will scam you. Your local Better Business Bureau office can help you, but the Attorney General's Office is best source of information regarding complaints and legal actions against a company.

If you want to try to fix your credit yourself, the Federal Trade Commission has excellent resources available online at: *www.FTC.gov*. The FTC publishes a 24-page booklet entitled *Building A Better Credit Report* which is very helpful. That booklet is available on the Free Downloads page of my website at www.CreatingFinancialLiteracyLLC.com. However, repairing your own credit is time consuming and requires ongoing follow up both by mail and telephone.

If you want a reputable company to handle your credit restoration process, provide you with guidance related to increasing your credit score, and also show you how to pay down any debts faster, go to: *www.RetiredYoungAndHappy.com*. Watch the 6-minute video. If you request additional information at the end of the video, your request will come directly to my office. Please include your telephone number and someone in my office will contact you. If you choose to use the debt elimination program described in the video, you will also get absolutely free credit restoration services for both you and your spouse included with the program! Remember that 30% of your credit score is paying down your debts!

This is the only one of the 12 Money Opportunities that will not produce an immediate monthly financial savings. However, in the long run, increasing your credit scores could save you more money over time than all other 11 Money Opportunities combined! How? Because with high credit scores, you have the opportunity to call your creditors and ask them to lower your current interest rates; obtain mortgages at the best rates; and leverage your credit scores for other opportunities.

You still need to go to the Money Opportunity Log at the end of this book and track this Money Opportunity. Write Yes or No in the space if you have your current credit report (less than 6 months old) and credit score. Put a star (*) next to this opportunity if your credit scores are over 700 or if you have already taken action steps to get your scores up over 700. Our office periodically offers workshops on increasing credit scores and other financial topics. The workshops are listed online at *www.CreatingFinancialLiteracyLLC.com*.

IMPORTANT NOTE: It is critically important that all 17 year old children in your life pull their credit reports about 6 months before their 18th birthday. These 17 year olds may be your children, family members, family friends, church members, etc. Why is this so important? Because too many children are victims of identity theft and it's much easier to clear errors on their credit reports before they turn 18.

Unfortunately, in this economy some adults are putting items like phones, utilities, and more in the names of children. This is often done with the best intentions of paying the bills, but perhaps the house is going into foreclosure or the adult gets laid off or any number of financial interferences.

Children don't usually find out that bills have been put into their name until it's too late. They may get turned down for an apartment, a car loan, or even lose a job offer because of items on their credit reports that are not theirs. These turn downs usually occur after their 18th birthday. Once a child turns 18, the incorrect information on their credit reports is much, much harder to remove! These kids' credit histories are ruined for several years due to something they had no knowledge of!

So again, I must encourage you to have all the 17 year olds in your life pull their credit report several months before their 18th birthday. Just like you, they can pull their credit reports at www.AnnualCreditReport.com. Hopefully the inquiry will come back saying something along the lines of "no report found", meaning there is no credit established in that person's name. However, some kids have cell phones in their own name. If that's the case, the phone and any other legitimate items may appear on their credit report.

Money Opportunity #7
Adjust Withholdings

I call this your "instant pay raise"! This is a HUGE Money Opportunity that can create a few hundred dollars every month by itself! Every time you get paid, the government takes what it believes is its fair share of *your* hard earned money first, which is at least 15%!

Billions of workers simply accept this loss of cash without doing anything about it. And, when tax refund checks are received each spring, people get excited about getting their own money back! However, the truth is that refund checks are nothing more than what's left over after you make an interest free loan to the government, and some people pay extra to get their own money back by using refund anticipation loans!

If you are like most people, you over pay in taxes. You give a guy named Sam (my Uncle would never take money from me like this!) an interest free loan for 12 months. Then, every spring you wait with excitement and anticipation for this guy Sam to give you *some* of your money back! Really, it is just *some* of your money! Look on your W-2 to see how much money you loaned Sam without any interest, and compare it to how much you got back. There's no reason to give that guy Sam an interest free loan, especially if you're struggling to make it from one payday to the next!

Look at these numbers... If you get a $1,200 tax refund check, that's $100 each month ($1,200/12 months) that your accountant could possibly help you get legally added to your paycheck every month. If you get paid twice a month or every other week, a $1,200 tax refund check amounts to about $50 in each paycheck! If your refund check is usually $2,400, you could get $200 per month.

For this Money Opportunity, talk to your professional tax preparer, who is preferably an accountant, to see if you can adjust your withholdings to get more of your money in every paycheck. You should discuss scenarios that will leave you with a small refund, say $500 or less so that you do not owe the IRS when you file your taxes. There are websites with withholding calculators; however, if you make a mistake you can end up owing the IRS.

Also, it is very important that if you adjust your withholdings that you take the extra money from every paycheck and faithfully put it into one of your savings or investment accounts. To help make sure you consistently save this extra money from every paycheck, set up an automatic transfer to move the money into your savings account on your payday. These transfers are very, very easy to set up. Research which financial institutions, both online and walk in, offer the best interest rates.

Some people are OK with overpaying in taxes every year to get a big refund check because they do not believe they have the self-discipline to faithfully save the extra money from each paycheck. This book is basically about changing thoughts and habits like these because they are holding you back from your total financial success. Adjusting your withholdings and saving money every month earns interest for you each month for 12 months, which will create more money in your bank account after 12 months than if you just get it at one time from the IRS without any interest.

Remember, I told you this book contains 12 simple steps and that some of them would get you more than $20 per month! Contact a tax professional to determine what adjustments you need to make with your employer to get your money today and still not owe the IRS in April. The bonus chapter will explain what you can do to make your refund check even bigger! Imagine what will happen to your financial challenges after consistently applying everything in this book, and then getting a bigger refund check because you implemented some or all of the bonuses at the end of the book!

Go to the Money Opportunity Log at the end of this book and write in the amount of money created by adjusting your withholdings. Did Money Opportunity #7 double what was created in the first six Opportunities combined? For some of you it did! Congratulations to everyone!

Author's Note: This Money Opportunity is not about avoiding taxes or doing anything illegal. In these tough economic times, some families actually need their tax money every month for their basic survival, instead of waiting until March or April for a lump sum check. With the high unemployment rate and many two income homes now surviving on one income, an extra $100 or $200 every month could make a big difference for many families across the country.

Money Opportunity #8
Cable/Pay TV

You probably realized that if you can lower your electric bill by turning the television off one extra hour each day in Money Opportunity #4, then at some point I would suggest getting rid of paid television all together! Don't worry! The pangs in your heart at the thought of no cable will go away – I promise!

I realize this is a radical thought, but take a few minutes to truly analyze what you actually get for the $30 – $200 you spend every month just to watch TV vs. how $30 – $200 every month will help you get over your financial hurdles. Of course, I don't buy into the excuse of needing to pay for television to get TV reception. Even with the DTV switch, a $40 converter box is all you need.

What you get with cable is entertainment, not empowering education. Plus, you and your family also get constantly bombarded with advertising messages to spend money that you really don't have, or that is better spent on something else like college savings, homeownership, or retirement funds. Yes, there are some educational channels on pay television, but I'm asking you to look at the channels that are watched in *your* home. Plus, how much time do you spend in front of the TV? What about the amount of time your children spend? Does your family spend more time watching TV than relaxing, learning, and exploring through reading?

51

Did you know that by the time the average child starts 1st grade, they have spent half their life in front of the television?[2] That's 3 full years of TV watching for these 6 year old children! In 2007, American adults and teens spent an estimated 3,518 hours watching, which is nearly five months each.[3]

On top of the time wasted watching TV, an average of $936 per person per year is spent on purchasing items viewed in the media.[4] For a family of four, that's nearly $4,000 buying what was seen on TV and cable. Plus, if your cable bill is $100/mo, you actually paid $1,200 to watch the ads that convinced you to spend the $4,000! That's $5,200 per year, which is $100 spent each and every week because of television!

The time you and your children spend watching television replaces quality family and learning time with luring advertisements; cartoons; sexually explicit images, lyrics, and language; violent images and other things that do absolutely nothing to promote your personal, professional, financial, and/or family growth.

If you are serious about changing your financial future and are serious about achieving your financial goals, yet still see an absolute need to pay to have television in your home, then look

[2] Abandoned in the Wasteland: Children, Television and the First Amendment, by Newton Minnow, former Chairman of the FCC, and Craig LaMay, 1995
[3] US Census Bureau's Statistical Abstract of the United States: 2007: "Media Usage and Consumer Spending: 2000 to 2009."
[4] Ibid.

for ways to at least cut the cable bill in half by asking yourself these simple questions:

- Do my children *need* paid TV in their bedroom? Note: if your children are not straight A/B students, totally removing the television from their bedroom may be an educational opportunity in addition to a Money Opportunity
- Can I return all the cable boxes except for the one in the living room or family room?
- Can I reduce my TV service to the most basic plan?
- Can I eliminate paid TV service or at least reduce it to the most basic service for one year, perhaps only increasing my channels during special times such as one sport season to get all the games, or only have it during the summer when the kids don't have homework?
- If I live in a rural area where I honestly may need to pay to get regular TV reception, what is the best deal my telephone and cable providers have for this type of service? What will a one-time fee for a DTV converter box do for my finances instead of an ongoing, recurring monthly bill. Note: Cable service to simply provide for television reception typically costs less than $25 per month. You probably have to ask for this service because it is usually not advertised or readily offered.

Even if you only turn the paid TV service off for 6 months, perhaps during the school year, think of how much money you can save and how much information you and your children can read and learn with your new free time! Think about how much time you will now have with your family for interaction, fun, and exploring new interests.

Underscoring the importance of not having cable or regular TV as available to your children is the fact that more children in

America can quote more song lyrics than words in their schoolbooks! They know more TV shows than poetry, math formulas, or...ways to manage money! Remember that by the time the average child enters 1st grade they have watched an average of 3 years of television. At age six, they have literally spent half of their young lives in front of the TV...all during the time in their lives when they learn the most!

Between TV and text messaging, old-fashioned communication and family fun are being lost in many homes and in society. When you turn the television off and play educational and financial board games with your children, your children learn about entrepreneurship and how to manage money at an early age. When you talk with your children about their future, don't ask them what they want to be when they grow up, ask them what they want to own!

Your children can become doctors, but they need to OWN the medical practice. They can become bus or truck drivers, but they need to OWN the fleet of vehicles. For example, I know a very successful woman who owns a tour bus company and does not have a Commercial Driver's License (CDL), which is required by law to drive the very buses she owns! Yet, that company has made her millions of dollars!

Every adult in America is watching the economy shift right before our eyes. For our children to effectively compete when their generation reaches adulthood, they need to understand and be educated about both money and entrepreneurship. Even though this book is about your personal finances and getting money for you right now, there is other very important information such as getting today's children ready to compete in tomorrow's economy.

With the current unemployment rate, many adults are exploring business ownership to make ends meet; recoup losses in the stock market; and more. However, imagine how much easier it would be if every adult had grown up learning about entrepreneurship and owning a business, and did not have to worry as much about layoffs, furloughs, and/or pay cuts? Teaching your children about money and entrepreneurship are life-long opportunities you can give them before they turn 18! Go to the Free Downloads page of my website, www.CreatingFinancialLiteracyLLC.com for a list of resources to help you teach your children about money. Encourage your children to play the money games that are also on the website.

With the TV turned off, talk openly with your children, nieces, and nephews about their future so they learn at an early age the value of combining formal education and informal education (i.e. books, internships, and workshops) with entrepreneurship. Also understand that it is not too late for you to own your own business, even if it's a home-based business. We will explore the benefits of business ownership shortly, including some amazing tax benefits you may not be aware of.

Go to the Money Opportunity Log at the end of this book and write in the amount of money created by cancelling or scaling back on your paid television bill. Were you able to turn off your cable or at least create $20 each month? Excellent! Many of you are probably unbelievably excited because your Money Opportunity Log is already totaling more than $400 or $500 that you have created every month! Congratulations to you!

Money Opportunity #9
Personal Care, Insurance, and Banking

Personal care is another category that usually creates more than $20 in Money Opportunities every month. Personal care includes things like hair, nails, massages, and other personal care. However, this category is definitely not just for the ladies! Men may not spend as much on personal care as their female counterparts, but men have gym memberships, haircuts, shaves, mustache trims, and other grooming expenses.

The bottom line is to create a minimum of $20 in this category, which may simply mean eliminating one personal care service each month. This can be done by performing the service yourself or bartering with a friend. Ladies and men, you will both still look fantastic after creating money in this Opportunity!

Insurance is a necessity. Different insurances you may need include car, homeowner, renter, life, and others. Insurance is included in this book because it's critically important to shop around and compare rates. If you have a mortgage, homeowner insurance is required. If you rent, renter's insurance may not be required by the property owner; however, *every renter should have renter's insurance.*

Renter's insurance could cost as little as $10 per month. For that small amount of money, your belongings are covered if there is a fire, theft, or other damage. Many policies cover the cost to replace what was damaged or destroyed after you pay a small deductible. Imagine your neighbor left an unattended pot on the stove and the fire damaged your apartment. Depending on your renter's policy, your insurance company would pay for your clothes, furniture, electronics, and more to be cleaned or replaced, plus they may pay for temporary housing while your apartment is being repaired. All of this for as little as $10 per month, and you know that the contents of your apartment are worth far more than $10!

It is important to shop around and compare prices from different insurance companies. Most insurance companies will give a discount if you have more than one policy with them (i.e. home or renter insurance plus car or life insurance). Remember that low credit scores can mean higher insurance premiums; however, you still need to get each of the types of insurance you need to protect yourself and your family. As your credit scores increase, you can let the insurance companies know and they may lower your rate.

For some people, banking has become a costly expense. Take time to review your bank statements from the past few months. Do you see any fees? If so, how much do you spend each month in bank fees? Is your bank considering charging new fees such as a fee to use your debit card? What is the interest rate on savings, money market, and other accounts?

The easiest banking fee to get rid of is the overdraft or bounced check charge. This fee can be $40 or more, and some people bounce checks (plural!) every month. Start balancing your checkbook daily and transfer what you usually pay in monthly bounced check fees into your savings account!

Since the credit card reform act became law, some banks have been eliminating standard services such as free checking. Additionally, some banks have started charging fees for things that were previously free. So far, credit unions do not charge as many fees as some banks may charge. Credit unions have members, and there are simple rules regarding who is eligible to join, such as living or working in a particular area.

If your bank has recently started charging fees for services that were previously free, make a list of the credit unions and other banks in your area. Call or visit a branch and ask if they charge fees for services comparable to what you currently get from your bank. If it is a credit union, ask if you meet the membership criteria. If your research identifies a credit union or bank that will charge you less fees for the same or similar types of accounts that you currently have, consider switching. Put the amount you save in reduced fees each month into one of the accounts you open!

Go to the Money Opportunity Log at the end of this book and write in the amount of money created from changes to personal care expenses; by shopping around for the best insurance prices; and by eliminating bank fees.

Money Opportunity #10
Luxuries and Liabilities

This Money Opportunity can put lots of money in your pocket! In most months, people spend significant amounts of money on small and medium-sized items that add up quickly! "Liabilities" is purposely in the title of this Money Opportunity. A liability is any purchase that costs money and does not put money in your pocket.

Liabilities can include large electronic purchases, cars, and more. Even though a car may be a necessity, it does not generate income for most people; therefore, it is actually a liability. Unfortunately, some people buy larger, more luxurious, or fully equipped cars with all the bells and whistles when the truth is they really cannot afford them.

On a regular basis it's the smaller, sometimes ongoing purchases that slowly ease us into financial trouble, and present an Opportunity for adjustment. Men may purchase CDs, DVDs, music downloads, and video games to add to their collections. There are also small and medium-sized electronics purchases, and accessories for those items. Some men put lots of money into their cars in items such as rims, detailing, sound systems, and other "toys and gadgets." And fellas, what would life be like without your favorite video games?!

Ladies, of course we must start with clothes, shoes, and purses! And, the perfect outfit is not complete without jewelry and make up. Remember to add the expense of the outing where the outfit will be worn! Those expenses may include the ticket, dinner, drinks, and more.

For both men and women, the above shopping purchases should be put on the scale of needs vs. wants. Until your finances improve, only buy what you truly need. Lots of people are staying in financial trouble longer than necessary because they choose to spend money to buy "wants" and non-necessities.

I'm not saying don't get dressed up or don't go out. However, I am saying think about the pros and cons of the total cost of the outing given where you are financially. This includes social outings like girls' night out, hanging with the fellas, and happy hour. For me, I have to monitor football season. I have to go to a bar or restaurant to see my favorite team play because they are not local. I actually limit the number of games I watch and I adjust my spending plan to allow for these costs during football season.

Often, these unnecessary purchases give us instant gratification and immediate happiness. What we should be doing is staying strong and true to ourselves by holding off on these purchases and practicing delayed gratification so that we have money for bills, savings, or larger purchases. The ongoing purchases of non-necessities often become spending habits that cause us financial stress. This is also a habit we pass on to our children, and it sets them up for financial challenges.

Other luxuries that present us with a Money adjustment may include housecleaning services cleaning, pet sitting, and other services that, yourself, may be the difference between needing a part-time and not needing one.

Understand that even the smallest purchase, if bought with credit and not paid in full before interest accrues, can end up costing hundreds and even thousands of dollars by the time it's paid off! For example, a $20 purchase (i.e. a CD) each bi-weekly payday is $520 over the course of 12 months. If those purchases are made with credit cards and not paid off at the end of every month, interest will accrue and take the total cost of those small, seemingly insignificant purchases to well over $600! A single $200 purchase on a credit card at 18% interest and paying the monthly minimum due can cost $239...and that's only if you do not charge anything else on that credit card! A $3,500 television at 18% interest can cost an additional $2,015 for a total of $5,515, and will take 11 years to pay off!

There are several ways to create money with this Money Opportunity. First, look at your home and personal services and see which ones you can do yourself, at least for a few months or one year until you can breathe easier financially. Write the cost savings in your Money Opportunity Log. Next, when you are tempted to buy something – don't buy it! Go home and wait 2 or 3 days to see if you still feel that you must absolutely have the item in question. If you decide not to make the purchase, write he amount of the item in your Money Opportunity Log and transfer that amount of cash to your savings or investment account. If you cheat and go buy it next month, you have to subtract the amount from next month's savings!

Third, if you purchase the item and use credit, figure out on paper or with an online interest calculator how to pay off the item in the shortest time with the least amount of interest. Remember that paying your bills on time and paying down your credit card balances helps your credit scores. In your Money Opportunity Log, write the amount saved every month as you follow your steps to pay off the item faster.

Money Opportunity #11
The Power of Lists

The financial challenges associated with this category come from *not* using written lists and letting that power slip through your fingers...and your money right along with it! Putting money in your pocket with this Money Opportunity is easy. You simply use a written list for all of your shopping including groceries, holidays, birthdays, and special occasions. Knowing what you are buying from the grocery store, who you are buying for at gift time, and what your spending limits are at all times will create much more than $20 in this category, especially when buying items on sale.

By creating and using shopping and special occasion lists, you can clip coupons from newspapers and buy gifts on sale before the actual occasion. I never thought I had time to clip coupons until I worked in a supermarket. I was a cashier and watched people literally take as much as $200 off their grocery bills with coupons and sale items! I was truly amazed! Even as a single person there were times when I saved more than $30 on my grocery bill with coupons and sale items.

You never buy for the sake of buying just because something is on sale; however, taking a few minutes to look at the coupons and grocery store sales in your local newspaper can save you lots of money, and there are several reputable coupon websites. If you don't have time to clip coupons, let your children clip the coupons for items they like and that they know you purchase.

65

...ntly, there have been several TV shows dedicated to couponing. Search the internet for ideas on how to save money with coupons.

Another Money Opportunity is to purchase gifts in advance when you know someone is getting married or when someone's birthday is coming up. As you pass through stores, check the sale racks to see if there is something available that would make a great gift for someone on your list or for an upcoming occasion. Buy the item, put it away with the person's name on it, and mark the purchase off your list. Also watch the clearance page of your favorite store's website. You may be able to save money on gifts purchased online.

I actually have a "gift corner" in my home. I buy things all year round for people on my lists and put them in the corner. By October, I'm usually finished my holiday shopping and truly enjoy the season because I'm not forced into the hustle and bustle of malls, high prices, and rushed decision-making. By finishing my shopping in advance, I am not affected by advertisers or by stores that may raise prices so they can later mark them down, and then advertise the items as being on sale!

An example is if you regularly take a bottle of wine or house gift when visiting friends, and you make these visits a few times each year, you can buy the wine or house gift when you see good sales. That way, when friends have social gatherings at their homes, you can grab a bottle of wine off your rack or a house gift from your gift area and go without spending additional money that was not budgeted for!

This trick also works well if you have children. If you have children, keep extra age-appropriate toys in the house because children are usually invited to birthday parties on a regular basis. Select a toy from the shelf, wrap it, and off your child goes to the party without affecting your budget. Early January clearance sales are great sources for deals on toys!

Do you entertain often or snack a lot, especially during your favorite sports seasons or the backyard grilling season? Grab your non-perishable food items in advance when they are on sale, and if you have coupons it's an extra savings! These are several different examples of how using written lists to buy in advance can save money because you were able to plan ahead for the items you know you will need.

Right now, take the time to write the names of everyone you purchase birthday and holiday gifts for. Include their birth month, clothing size, and up to 5 things they would like to have. Make a copy of the list and keep it with you so that when you see something on sale that's on the list, you can purchase it, put it away with their name on it, and cross the person off the list.

Keep an ongoing grocery list on the refrigerator that everyone can add to as items run out. Watch out because little kids and big kids may like to sneak unnecessary items on the list from time to time! Just because something is on the list does not mean it must be purchased. Only spend what is budgeted for and let non-essential items stay on the list until there's extra money to cover the purchase. Remember to use your coupons!

In the Money Opportunity Log, enter the amount of money saved on your grocery bill this month using a written list and coupons, as compared to last month's grocery bill. In months where you purchase gifts on sale for people on your list, write the price difference between the regular price and the sale price in your Money Opportunity Log.

As months come and go, enjoy watching the amount of money you are able to put in your pocket grow every month by simply using written lists, clipping coupons, and watching the clearance aisle for gifts you know you can give to someone on your list.

Money Opportunity #12
Money Logging

You probably enjoyed flipping to the back of this book after each Money Opportunity and writing in the amount of money you put in your pocket from each adjustment. If you have been totally honest with yourself about what you really *need* to have vs. the things you *want*, then your Money Opportunity Log is already well over $240 and we still have one more Opportunity!

The last way to put money in your pocket every month without a part time job is actually one of the biggest! For this Money Opportunity, get a small 3x5 notebook to keep in your pocket or purse. In the notebook, you need to write down every penny you spend each and every day for a minimum of 60 days. Write every penny spent and every purchase made, from the gumball machine to your mortgage or rent! Include money given to your children, church, bills, etc.

At the end of every week, review the entries in your notebook and circle the items you can adjust next time. In the next week, work on adjusting each of the circled items while still recording each of your new purchases. Transfer the money created into your savings or investment account and record it in the Money Opportunity Log for this chapter.

Go back and review Money Opportunity #3 – Lunch and Snacks at Work to see some of the ways you previously spent money. This money logging exercise will show you other areas where you can put money in your pocket every month. Any money that leaves your hands, pocket, bank account, etc. is to be recorded in your notebook. This exercise will reveal your spending habits and any spending patterns. Once you see how you spend money, you can make plans and necessary changes accordingly.

As an example, if you buy water at the gym 3 days a week for $1.50 per bottle, then you can see the savings of buying a 24 bottle case of water at the store for $3.99. All you need to do is keep a bottle in your gym bag, and the $4 case of water will last through 24 workouts. In this example, buying 24 bottles of water at the gym ($1.50 each) is $36. Subtract the $4 you paid for the case of water at the store, and your Money Opportunity is $32!

Before you add the cash created from this opportunity in your Money Opportunity Log, take a few minutes to list the items that your notebook shows you spend the most money on. You may be able to group some spending into categories that you can work on adjusting.

This could be your biggest Money Opportunity! Take time to review your notebook. What does it reveal about how and where you spend money? For example, does your notebook reveal that you buy lots of books and magazines that you may be able to get from the library instead? Perhaps your notebook shows you that you give your children an allowance and then use your money instead of theirs for fast food, toys, and other things they want (not need)?

12 Ways To Put Money In Your Pocket Every Month

Use this space to write 10 items or areas from your 3x5 notebook that you now see you can create money from:

1._____

_____

2._____

_____

3._____

_____

4._____

_____

5._____

_____

6._____

_____

7._____

_____

8._____

_____

9._____

_____

10._____

_____

Go to the Money Opportunity Log at the end of the book and write in the amount of money created by tracking the money you spend every day.

Conclusion: Important Keys to Creating Your Better Life

You made it! Give yourself a hug and a pat on the back for making it to the end of this book and for putting so much of your own money back into your pocket! Understand the major financial accomplishments you made by allowing yourself to think differently and by taking the necessary steps to adjust your spending habits! Many of you used this book to uncover hundreds of dollars every month. For some of you, the amount of money you created equals what you could earn from a part-time job, except it did not cost you 20 hours of time away from your family to do it!

This book has shown you 12 Ways to Put Money in Your Pocket Every Month Without a Part-Time Job! Each Money Opportunity is simple, and some were easier than others to create money with. These Money Opportunities are designed to empower you to think about, address, and then resolve some of your financial opportunities and challenges. The 12 Ways you just read are very simple; however, the struggle for most people is with their willingness to change their priorities, habits, and mindsets.

Most people can't create the life they dream about because they feel closed in by their situations and circumstances, and money constraints are often a big factor. Simply having more money does not change your life. Money is a tool, and when it is used correctly, having more money simply allows you to have more options. It is the choices you make with your available options that allows you to pursue your dreams!

One of the key reasons for writing this book is to help you, the reader, to have extra cash so you have more options available to you. Making good, solid decisions with the extra money consistently available to you after reading this book is what leads you to improving your life on a sustained, long-term basis. The more money you can accumulate, the more choices (options) you will have. These options may be big or small. However, if you stop following the steps in this book or you constantly spend the extra money you create each month using this book, you will not accumulate enough cash to start giving yourself the long-term and long-lasting options you so desire.

If you held true to your original commitment you made to yourself at the beginning of this book, the money you logged after applying each of the 12 Money Opportunities should add up to at least $240, and probably much more. If you repeat your steps next month, you should save another $240 or more again. As you create money throughout each month, always remember to transfer the money into a separate savings account as it's created during the month. The key is to repeat your steps month after month after month, because it's not how much money you make but how much you keep that's important! You can print a Money Log every month so you can continue logging the money you create. A printable version of the Money Log is available on my website at www.CreatingFinancialLiteracyLLC.com.

Your Money Mindset

Taking control of your money is a process that takes time and practice. If you think about it, you did not walk perfectly with your first step as a baby. The same is true for your first time riding a bike, driving a car, success in your job, and more. Everything you now do well in your life took time to learn and time to practice. Just like you have mastered so many great things in your life, you will master managing your money if you stay with the process and vow to never give up!

Now that you have completed the 12 Money Opportunities, it's time to get down to the business of making the best choices for what to do with your extra money. After completing the steps in this book, you probably have more than $240 in extra money every month. I also hope you have thoughts and ideas about other Money Opportunities that may exist in your life. I encourage you to explore these additional Money Opportunities, and then take massive and immediate action to create even more cash for yourself, your family, and your future! One reader used the information in this book to think of other Money Opportunities in her life. She now has an extra $1,000 every month from the same job she's held for many years!

The thought processes and steps you took to complete each Money Opportunity should also have shown you possible underlying reasons for some of your financial challenges. Think about a few of the internal struggles and conversations you had with yourself about what or how much you could really adjust with some of the Money Opportunities. Did your inner voice try to talk you out of making some adjustments and try to rationalize some others? These thoughts may be clues as to why you spend money the way you do. Be honest with yourself as you reflect back on your thoughts because they are important as you keep working to apply what you learned in this book in the months and years to come.

The way you think about money is often referred to as your money mindset. This is how you consciously and subconsciously think and feel about money. Your money mindset usually goes back to your childhood and is based upon what adults around you said and did with their money. How you were raised regarding money is usually how you deal with money as an adult – and you may not even realize it!

For example, if you were raised in a home where there wasn't much money, as an adult you may hold on to your money very tightly because you're subconsciously afraid that you will run out of money and end up struggling and living without as you did in your childhood.

Perhaps you were raised in an environment where every time you asked for something you were told 'no' and you were constantly denied getting what you wanted. As a result when you become an adult, you may indulge yourself (or overindulge yourself) by buying whatever you and/or your family want. This spending pattern overcompensates for being repeatedly denied your wants and desires as a child.

76

Another example occurs when people were raised in environments where either you did not have "nice" things as child or you lived a lavish lifestyle with access to the best of everything. In both of these cases, both appearance and material possessions are often important as adults. Regardless of whether the adult can truly afford the appearance of luxury living, the luxurious purchases are often made anyway and a mountain of debt and stress often hangs over these households.

I encourage you to think about your childhood and the adults you were around. How did they feel about money? What money "messages" did they give you based upon their situations and circumstances? Can you see how your upbringing plays a role in your spending patterns and spending habits today?

Just like you learned your current money mindset, you can work to learn a new money mindset! The only thing that's required is an all out commitment to yourself and to creating the future you desire! Your new money mindset should be aligned with your current personal values and dreams. It will be very helpful to you to read positive, motivational magazines and books (see the Appendix at back of this book for a list). You may also choose to find several authors and/or motivational speakers that you identify with, and then follow their material.

Paid, Saved, and Gave

While you're working on changing your money mindset, there are simple steps you can take right now to move toward your goals and dreams with the money you just created from this book. If you think back to the *Forward* section of this book, where I shared my story, I mentioned dividing my paycheck into 3 categories: *Paid, Saved,* and *Gave.* These simple money categories may work for you just like the simplicity of the 12 Money Opportunities allowed you to create money.

Let's start with *Savings.* Savings is the most important category for your future goals and dreams! Saving as much of your extra money as possible will present you with options and opportunities for making your goals and dreams come true. In this economy, many people focus their attention on paying down debt and/or making ends meet. However, I want to keep encouraging you to balance these goals with increasing your savings.

Even though you may need the money created in this book to make ends meet, you still need to be saving systematically. Remember, until you read this book and started taking a hard look at where your money was going, you were living without this extra money you now have because it was being spent somewhere. Therefore, whether you are trying to make ends meet or your goal is getting out of debt, you need to have an equal focus on accumulating 6 – 12 months of living expenses in case something happens to your primary source of income.

Unless you are behind in your mortgage payments, you must absolutely leave a minimum of 1/3 of the money created with this book in a savings account or transfer it into an investment account *every month* (remember you were living without this money!). The best and easiest way to do this is through direct deposit or automatic transfers into an account that does not have an ATM card. For example, if you created $300 every month from the 12 Money Opportunities, you would leave at least $100 in a savings account for a total of $1,200 saved every year.

Depending upon your goals and dreams, you may decide to open several savings accounts and divide your deposits between them. The money deposited into each account is dedicated to a particular goal. For example, you may use one account for an emergency fund, one for a house down payment, one for retirement*, and one for vacation. If you are saving $150 each month, you may choose to put $40 into (each of) the emergency fund, house down payment, and retirement accounts, and the remaining $30 into the vacation account. If your bank or financial institution does not provide the ability to have multiple free savings accounts, look into an online bank. Online banks allow you to set up automatic transfer schedules to make it even easier to save. (*Note: You should meet with an experienced financial planner regarding the best retirement account for you based upon your age, goals, and other factors.)

If you are behind in your mortgage or think you may get behind, immediately go to the website for your state's department of housing. The website should have a list of approved non-profit housing counseling agencies that can help you explore mortgage and pre-foreclosure options. Another resource for pre-foreclosure assistance is: www.HUD.gov. Search their website for information on avoiding foreclosure, approved housing counseling agencies, and helpful information and resources. The non-profit mortgage assistance resources listed at HUD.gov and on your state's website do not charge fees for foreclosure assistance services.

The second of the three money categories is *Giving*. Regardless of your religious beliefs, giving is a critically important aspect in life that everyone should participate in. Giving of our time, talents, possessions, and our money to help someone or a cause we believe in actually makes the giver feel really good inside! No matter how tough or how tight things are in your home, many people are living in much tougher and much tighter situations.

From all of your income sources, set a goal to give a total of 10% to a church or non-profit organization that is meaningful to you. You may start out by giving less than 10%, while working your way up to a full 10% of your income. In the meantime, give of your time, talents, and possessions to a person or group in need. Do you have some gently used toys and/or household items that can be used by fire victims; by your local domestic violence shelter as they help women rebuild their lives; or by another group? Can you and your children draw pictures and sing songs together at a nursing home or on the children's floor at the hospital? Can you give blood, especially following a bad storm or during the summer when many regular blood donors are on vacation? What other talents do you have that you can share with others?

At some point in our lives, we all have benefited from the generosity of others. Giving to help make someone else's life easier and/or to bring a smile to their face gives us a good feeling inside. This is even more important for anyone who may be feeling down and out about their own personal situation. I challenge you to figure out ways to start giving to others right now, and I promise you that you will bring more happiness to yourself and your home in the process!

The third and final money category is *Paid*. Your paid category is where you saw all of your money going after you logged it in your 3x5 notebook during Money Opportunity #12. This is your biggest category and the category you need to continue watching closely! By now, you should be planning to save at least 1/3 of the extra money created using this book, and giving 10% of your total income away to a church or non-profit organization of your choice. Now it's time to focus on the bulk of your money and work on making decisions with that money that will allow your goals and dreams to come true!

Early in this book we used the example of planning a trip or special occasion, and stated the importance of planning how we spend all of our money. To better manage your money so that you can continue having more of it, use a monthly spending plan. A spending plan template is available on the Free Downloads page at: www.CreatingFinancialLiteracyLLC.com.

The 12 Money Opportunities and your 3x5 notebook will help you complete your spending plan. Keep using your spending plan and making adjustments to it every month until you start having money left over every month. It's OK if your first few spending plans are negative, meaning more bills and expenses than income. It is the practice and repetition of using the spending plan and making monthly adjustments that will change your outcome!

The ultimate goal is to always have more income than expenses every month so you can increase your savings and start making your goals and dreams come true! As this book proves, when people don't have a plan for how they spend their money, waste is created! Make an ongoing commitment to watching your paid category, using a spending plan every month, and keeping what you spend down to a minimum so that you can maximize your savings.

<u>Homeownership</u>

One of the best ways to stabilize your family and to accumulate wealth is through homeownership. If you do not own your home, consider homeownership. To buy a home you need steady income, good credit, and a down payment. Money Opportunity #6 addressed ways to increase your credit scores, and this entire book showed how to get money toward your down payment.

Start toward your homeownership goal right now by identifying one of your savings accounts for homeownership and systematically putting some of the money created using this book into that account every month. Next, ride by the outside of some starter homes in and around the area where you currently live. I purposely say "starter home" because your first house is rarely your dream house; it is usually a smaller home that is a stepping stone toward your dream home. Having a visual picture in your mind of what your new neighborhood and house may look like will help keep you focused on your homeownership goal because it may take a year or more to get there. However, it's worth the wait!

Early on the homeownership process, it is critically important that you figure out how much house you can truly and comfortably afford. The easiest way to figure out how much house you can afford is to start with how much you are currently paying in rent. Before you read this book and started having extra cash, did you absolutely and always pay your rent on time? Did you absolutely and always have enough money for your basic bills such as utilities, phone, transportation, and food?

If you answered 'yes' to each of these questions, then you can start with your current rent, and maybe even $100 – $200 more each month, as your ideal total mortgage payment. Your total mortgage payment consists of four parts: principal, interest, taxes, and insurance, and is sometimes referred to as PITI. To get an idea of the cost of homeowner's insurance, you can call the agent you purchased your renter's or car insurance through. Property taxes are listed on the information sheet about a house for sale.

It is important that you immediately start preparing for homeownership, if that's your goal! After determining how much you think you can afford for your mortgage payment, calculate the difference between that amount and how much you currently pay in rent. Then, faithfully start adding that difference to your homeownership savings account every month over and above what you are putting in there from the money created from this book. For example, if you think you want your mortgage payment to be $1,100 per month and your current rent is $950, you would add $150 per month to your savings account. At the end of 12 months of monthly deposits, you would have well over $1,800 toward your down payment!

Next, use an online mortgage calculator to figure out how much house you can afford based upon using your current rent as your PITI. For example, if you are considering a total mortgage payment of $1,100, then an affordable house for you would have a final sales price of about $180,000, and include a 5% down payment, seller assistance with closing costs, and $2,100 per year for taxes and insurance. This scenario would give you a total mortgage payment (PITI) of approximately $1,100.

Many non-profit housing counseling organizations have access to grant money that can be used toward your down payment and/or closing costs. Typically, you have to complete a series of homeownership classes (free) to get the money, and in most cases the money does not have to be paid back. To see a list of non-profit housing counseling organizations in the area in which you want to move, log on to www.HUD.gov. Also check with the human resources department where you work to see if your company offers programs to help employees buy homes.

<u>Your Challenge – A Money Smart Group</u>

Now that you have started the process of thinking differently about your money, and have enjoyed *immediate financial benefits*, make a commitment to yourself that you will continue to learn and grow financially! I challenge you to start a Money Smart Group. A Money Smart Group is a group of friends, coworkers, or family members who hold each other accountable to their ongoing savings using this book as a guide. You also celebrate each other's money victories! A money victory could be saving enough to reach your goal, or simply having the will power not to buy something that's just a want and not a true need.

Start your Money Smart Group right now by calling and emailing your potential group members to see who wants to participate. You can start by telling them how this book helped you, and then encourage them to buy the book and join your Money Smart Group. The book is available online at www.MoneySmartBook.com and on Amazon.

Once your Money Smart Group members have their copy of the book, you are on your way to having a support system in place to help make sure you reach your goals! You can also set up friendly competitions within your Money Smart Group to see who saves the most each month or see who only uses cash for holiday purchases. The winner achieves their goals and dreams as their prize! Email me at Jennifer@12WaysBook.com about your Money Smart Group and I will gladly participate by phone in one of your check in meetings.

Thank you for having faith in me and faith in the title of this book. I trust that you found ways to create extra money for yourself and your family every month. I also hope that you will continue along your new path and continue to better manage your money and save toward your goals and dreams. The pages that follow are little "extras" that will help sustain and/or fast forward the financial portions of your goals and dreams, so keep reading!

Congratulations on your success and for taking major steps toward creating your new financial future!

BONUS #1
Your Next Step: Financial Self-Defense

Just by getting to this point in this book, I know you have made a strong commitment to making changes today that will benefit you financially in the long run, and that you are serious about achieving your goals and dreams! The next step for you is to consider putting a financial self-defense program in place that will reinforce the work you did while reading this book and to help you create a plan to reach your goals and dreams.

So, what is a financial self-defense program? It is a program that gives you complete access to a team of financial experts and systems that will help keep you on the right track and help your finances continue to grow. The financial self-defense program covers three key areas:

1. A written plan that shows you how to get out of debt as quickly as possible
2. Financial mentoring on any topic related to money such as retirement planning, college savings, taxes, budgeting, money management, and more
3. Professional credit restoration that averages increases of 50 – 150 points in credit scores

If you are really serious about continuing to do better financially, I suggest investing some of the money you created from this book into yourself and your future by enrolling in the financial self-defense program for 6 to 12 months, or even longer. Financial self-defense is good for everyone, especially in this economy. This program will help you continue on your road to greater financial success!

If one of your goals is to buy a house and you're not sure about your credit scores and/or you want to get rid of some of your debt before getting your mortgage, then you definitely want to invest in the financial self-defense program! If you are within ten years of retirement and want to retire with as little debt as possible and little or no time remaining on your mortgage, and/or you want to make sure you have enough money saved for your planned lifestyle as a retiree, then the financial self-defense program is perfect for you too!

At the time this book went into print, the cost of the financial self-defense program was only $69.95 per month, with a one-time set up charge of $14.95. Since you now have an extra $240 or more each month, there is $69.95 available to invest in sustaining and growing your finances for your future! And, if you are legally married, the $69.95 covers your spouse too! Simply call my office at 877-279-2701 or send an email to *Jennifer@12WaysBook.com* and someone will gladly answer your questions and get you enrolled into the financial self-defense program. There are no time commitments or contracts with the financial self-defense program, and you are free to cancel at any time!

BONUS #2
Making Extra Cash

Over the past few years, many people have experienced reductions in income through job loss, furlough days, and other reasons. Even after reading this book, some people will still struggle. In the *Giving* section of the Conclusion, I asked this question "what other talents do you have that you can share with others?" When I asked the question then, I was referring to donating your time and talents to an organization (which you should still do).

Now, I ask the same question here, "what other talents do you have that you can share with others"? This time, I want to know who will pay you to provide that service? Are you a great singer? Are good at scrapbooking, photography, or another hobby or activity?

I call this strategy "raising the rent". It simply involves letting people know what services you can provide for them for a fee. You may or may not make enough money to retire on, but if you make a few hundred dollars every month to pay the rent, utilities, or some other bill, your life will have less stress! Another great option for "raising the rent" is to sell items you are no longer using, perhaps at a yard sale, flea market, or online.

To start making extra cash using your talents and interests, write a list of things everything you love to do. As you write your list, don't worry about whether people will pay you to do those things – we'll deal with that in a moment. After you write this list, start a second list of things you can do to help others. Some examples include:

- Washing cars
- Baby sitting
- Cutting grass and shoveling snow
- Cutting and/or styling hair
- Wrapping gifts
- House cleaning
- Painting
- Grocery shopping and errands

There are many, many things you can do that someone else would pay you for. This is a very short list, and your list is as long as your imagination! Make a price list for each service so you know what you will charge when people contact you. Once you have your lists, make phone calls and send out flyers letting people know what you can do for them. For example, if you are a good singer, you may want to let churches and funeral homes know that you are available to sing at weddings and funerals. When you drop off your flyers with your contact information on them, you may want to sing a few lines for the person working there so they can hear how great you are!

The key to success in making extra cash with your talents is to always be honest, be professional, be creative, show up on time, and follow up. By following up I mean to return all phone calls within 24 hours, call ahead to confirm your scheduled services, and call after you finished to say "thank you" no matter how large or how small the job was!

BONUS #3
Money Creator: Increasing Your Tax Refund

The secret to increasing your tax refund is actually not a secret at all; it simply requires a good strategy! In the workplace, if you are in management you create strategies to run, grow, and generate profits for your company. If you are an employee, you do what management tells you so that the strategies they created make money for the company. This is true if the company is for-profit, non-profit, or government.

However, when most people leave work and go home, they do not have a strategy in place at home to make money or make the most of their money to benefit their family. In this economy (and any economy), everyone needs to have a home-based business as a strategy to increase their refund check.

Even after taking action on Money Opportunity #7, there is much more that can be done when it comes to taxes. Tax dollars that you do not get back will stay in the system. The government definitely needs money generated by taxes to run; however, having a legitimate home-based business can give you some say in how much of *your* tax dollars you will contribute.

As an example, if your household taxable income is $100,000, you are in the 28% tax bracket and will have about $28,000 in taxes deducted by your employer. If the typical refund check is $3,000, then $25,000 of your hard earned money is your contribution to the government.

Taxable Income	Tax Bracket	Estimated Taxes Paid
$33,000	15%	$4,950
$34,000	25%	$8,500
$60,000	25%	$15,000

As I revise this book in the midst of the worst economic downturn since the depression, the question I ask you is: *Where do you want your tax dollars to go? Wall Street? Main Street? or Your Address on Your Street?*

Money Opportunity #7 closed with mentioning that it's not too late for you to start your own business. Starting a real business is much different that using your talents and interests to hustle up some extra cash to help make ends meet. With an investment of time and effort on your part, a home-based business can provide you with a few hundred dollars a month or more in additional income, *and* possibly 4-figures or more *added* to your refund check! How?

People who own a home-based business on either a part-time or full-time basis have more than 125 tax deductions available to them that people who do not have a business cannot consider. To be eligible for any of the deductions, you must first have a qualifying home-based business, and then work in your business to meet the IRS definition of "intent to profit". A Certified Public Accountant (CPA), who has expertise in home-based business taxes, can help you understand the requirements. For the potential tax savings and extra income earned, the amount a qualified accountant charges is well worth it – and their fee is a tax deductible business expense!

The tax advantages alone make owning a home-based business something that *everyone* needs to have strategically. These tax advantages often allow you to write off "anyway" expenses. An "anyway" expense is something you would pay for anyway, that may now be tax deductible if you have a home-based business. Examples of some "anyway" expenses that may be tax deductible if you have a qualifying business include:

- A portion of your actual monthly mortgage or rent payment
- A portion of living expenses such as utility bills, phone bills, and more
- Some mileage
- Your children between the ages of 7 and 17, if you hire them to work in your home based business. The deduction has been over $5,000 per child in addition to the dependent deduction, and could be available even if a parent does not have custody
- Some meals and trips may also be deductible if they are related to your business

Think about this...if your home office space is 10% of your apartment or house and you pay $1,000 each month for rent or mortgage, you may be able write off $100 per month (10% of the payment), which adds up to $1,200 per year. Plus, you may be able to write off 10% of your utility bills to cover heating and cooling your home office space, along with some computer supplies, internet service, and telephone charges! The ongoing expenses listed in this paragraph are things you would pay for "anyway" that may become legal tax deductions if you had a qualifying home-based business as a strategy for your family.

If you have a child between the ages of 7 and 17 who can take phone messages, stuff envelopes and packages, hand out flyers, etc., then your deduction could be over $5,000. If you have three children in that age group, the deductions could add up to more than $15,000 if you hire them! These employed children are given a salary, which is a tax deductible business expense, instead of an allowance. The simple examples in these two paragraphs can add up to more than $17,000 in tax deductions for things you would pay for "anyway"! ...talk about the ultimate Money Opportunity!

I am not an accountant or tax professional and I do not provide any tax, legal, or other professional advice. It is critical that you check with a tax professional (preferably a CPA) who is experienced in home-based business taxes to learn which of the available deductions you can take, and how to keep the appropriate records needed to prepare your tax return. Can you see how owning a home-based business can make all or parts of some expenses you already pay tax deductible?! For more info on using a home-based business as a strategy to get a bigger refund check, go to: www.BiggerRefundCheck.com

Many people do not have the motivation, drive or true desire required to diligently research, start, operate, and grow a traditional business as an entrepreneur. It is because of this fact that I like sharing the simplicity of multi-level marketing and/or direct sales. In many instances, you only have to join your selected company as a representative, and then market their products and/or services, to have a business that can make you eligible for the tax deductions. There is usually a low start up cost (under $500), and the monthly cost of operating your business is also low, perhaps $50 per month or less. These costs are often tax deductible.

For those of you who have concerns about MLM/Multi Level Marketing (or Network Marketing) companies, remember this is simply part of your larger strategy, which is to create more cash at home. MLMs have been tested in court over and over. The courts have ruled many times that these companies provide a legitimate way to distribute products, and that the businesses are not pyramid or ponzi schemes. In fact, many retailers you are probably familiar with offer affiliate commissions and marketing opportunities to customers using the MLM concept, and some use the court-tested MLM wording.

Don't believe me? Look at the websites for Best Buy™, Toys R Us™, Amazon.com™, and other major retailers. Scroll to the bottom of the home page and find the link to their "affiliate" marketing opportunity. Once you find it, read how the company will pay you a commission for qualified sales based upon your referrals. That's the same way MLM companies pay their marketers! Several billionaire investors we regularly hear about in the news and see on TV are actively involved in, or own, MLM companies.

A handful of you are now saying you don't like selling and don't want to do this. However, if you see a good movie or visit a great restaurant, you probably tell/sell your friends to check it out. On the other hand, I bet that there are parts of your job or daily routines in your life that you don't like. Yet, you still go to work every day and create or implement strategies that create wealth for someone else. The point is to do *something* legally as a home-based business to get as many of your tax dollars back as possible, even if it's not an MLM or direct sales company!

For those of you thinking about writing a business plan and legally incorporating a small business in your state, I still recommend that you be strategic and join an MLM or direct sales company. Why? Because while you are taking the necessary time to do the research for your business plan, get business licenses, equipment, and other materials, the MLM could qualify you for tax deductions. The extra money generated from your sales and the extra money in your refund check could cover all or part of the start up costs for your dream business when you're ready to launch! Good MLM/direct sales companies also offer excellent sales and marketing training that may help you when you are ready to open your small business. Plus, your active involvement in your selected MLM/direct sales company may put you in position to meet people who can help your dream business get off the ground and grow!

This entire book is about improving your daily finances to put money in your pocket. If you do not already have a home-based business, there is one to research and consider because the products and services support your commitment to yourself to keep growing your finances. If you like the sound of a home-based business as a strategy, and would like to have me as one of your personal mentors in an MLM business, I encourage you to look at my website at www.EndYourRatRace.com.

If you like what you see and/or you want more information, call my office at 877-279-2701. We will help you get started and meet the 'intent to profit' rule. You tell us if you want to start your business slowly, perhaps only earning a few hundred dollars every week to offset the rising cost of living; or move quickly by working hard to earn thousands each month. You can achieve success regardless of your age or education level because training and support are provided to you. You only need to bring determination, persistence, and patience to your business!

Money Opportunity #7 looked at what you currently pay in taxes and provided a way to put some of your tax money into your pocket every month by adjusting your withholdings. Once you select an MLM or direct sales company and/or start your own business at home, the more than 125 home-based business tax deductions may even make some of the purchases you logged in Money Opportunity #12 tax deductible!

Remember that your employer pays you to create or implement strategies at work that make them money. Explore your home-based business options so that you can get started now doing what it takes as part of your strategy at home to have more money! Doing this will allow you to put the money you earn from your business directly into your pocket. Your home-based business money is in addition to the money you created from all of the Money Opportunities in this book, plus you will get the tax advantages every year!

Having a home-based business is not a job or a chore – it's a strategy! You work for yourself as the CEO of your own company. You control your income and your taxes so that you can invest in your future!

BONUS #4
Money Opportunity Hot Tips

Groceries: Buy a $25 gift card to your primary supermarket and keep it in your wallet or a safe place. If there ever comes a time that you or a family member is cash strapped and needs staples (i.e. milk, eggs, bread, etc.) use the gift card to get over the financial hurdle. NOTE: Make sure the gift card does not expire or have any fees attached.

Newlywed Couples: If you are getting married or recently got married, and one of you moved in with the other, you created a great Money Opportunity! When you combine households, you take two incomes into one home that was already being supported by one income. With some planning and a little hard work, you should be able to live on the one salary of the person who was already taking care of the home's expenses, and put 100% of the other person's salary into savings. If you truly cannot save 100% of the other salary, figure out how to save at least save 75%. Start by saving the amount the other person was paying for rent/mortgage, utilities, and insurance, and increase the monthly savings from there until you are saving 75-100% of the second income.

For newlyweds this is an awesome Money Opportunity because it is an opportunity to take the financial pressure off your marriage! The money saved can provide you with quick down payment money for a house, or money to set aside for when you have children and the wife is out of work for 6 – 12 weeks or more. As a couple, write down your goals and meet with a financial planner to discuss how to make the money you are saving achieve your goals.

Empty Nest Couples: Empty nest couples have an opportunity similar to newlyweds. In your case, the children are gone; therefore, your household expenses should be lower. Your goal is the same: start living on one salary. Meet with a financial planner and see if the saved income is best applied to increasing your retirement accounts, paying off your mortgage (remember to create a property tax fund and add 1/12 of your taxes each month), or another goal that you and your spouse may have. If you can start living on one income before retirement, the decrease in your post-retirement income won't seem as bad!

Family Lists: Money Opportunity #11 shared the power of using lists for purchases. This Hot Tip is to create lists of things to do for fun with your family. Make sure the list includes inside activities for cold or rainy days, and outside activities for better weather. Let everyone in your home make their own list and then combine them into one big list. These are great things to do while the TV is turned off and that time off is saving you 30 hours on your electric bill! Here are some ideas to get you started...

- Things to do and places to go that cost little or no money. Sign up for the weekly email blast from your local newspaper's entertainment section. Also sign up for the events e-blast for the largest town or city near you.

- Purchase board games and other activities on clearance sale at your local toy store.

- Start a toy and game swap with friends so that there are always "new" games to play.

- If you enjoy hanging out, make a list of all the restaurants with happy hour specials. Some specials include deep discounts on food and drinks. Meet your friends at different places on your list for low cost fun.

- Plan a trip to Washington, DC. DC is full of monuments and museums and most of them do not charge admission, including the many Smithsonian museums and The National Zoo! DC is also famous for "pay what you can" nights at many theatres including the Kennedy Center. On these special nights, you literally pay what you want at the door! Check your town to see if your local theatres have "pay what you can" night, or maybe even free admission to a dress rehearsal before the show opens.

- Join zoos and museums that offer reciprocal memberships. This is a secret gem! Some zoos and museums around the country have relationships with others that will let their members into each other's museums and zoos for free! Do your homework and consider purchasing a family membership at the least expensive venue, and then use that membership at all the locations that will accept it. For more information go to: http://www.childrensmuseums.org/visit/reciprocal.htm and http://www.astc.org/members/passlist.htm for two examples. Use the internet to find more.

- Research which beaches and amusement parks offer annual season passes. In addition to annual passes, some amusement parks allow you to buy tickets years in advance to lock in the current season's ticket price. Walt Disney World™ is one example. There are some restrictions, but if you know you plan on taking the family in a few years, you may consider using some of your Money Opportunity savings to buy passes at the current park admission prices. Note: if advance purchase tickets are lost they usually cannot be replaced.

- Use the internet to search out more great activities for your list, and remember to let everyone create their own list of ideas and activities!

We want to hear from you! Email us how much you created with your Money Opportunities and what great activities are on your list. Include your name, city, and telephone number. Send your email today to jennifer@12waysbook.com

APPENDIX A
Resources for Your Continued Growth

If you enjoyed watching the money in your Money Opportunity Log add up, and you want be able to put more and more money into your pocket every month, then you need to read and study financially empowering books, articles, and other literature to better understand money and cash flow. As your knowledge and awareness about money grows, you will begin to see even more Money Opportunities in your life that are not listed in this book! Remember what my mentor taught me – *money is just an idea and people who lack money simply lack ideas!*

Successful people do what unsuccessful people will not do. Unsuccessful people will not sit down and face their problems, especially digging into their thoughts and situations to get to the root causes of their financial problems. Successful people like you are willing to take massive and immediate action toward positive changes in their lives!

Dust off your library card and commit to reading six financial books and six personal development books each year (an average of one book each month). Here are some books and magazines to get you started or help you continue on your road to financial success, and toward achieving your vision.

Magazines
Success Magazine
Black Enterprise
Kiplinger's Personal Finance
Smart Money Magazine

Books about Money
The Wealth Cure by Hill Harper
The Millionaire Next Door by Thomas Stanley
The One Minute Millionaire by Mark Victor Hansen and Robert G. Allen

Books about Mindset
Rich Dad Poor Dad by Robert Kiyosaki and Sharon L. Lechter
Secrets of the Millionaire Mind by T. Harv Eker
What Makes the Great Great by Dennis Kimbro
Reallionaire by Farrah Gray
Three Feet From Gold by Sharon L. Lechter and Greg S. Reid
Eat That Frog by Brian Tracy
No Excuses by Brian Tracy

Books to Grow Your Business (Entrepreneurship)
Get More Clients Now by J.C. Hayden
Go For No by Richard Fenton and Andrea Waltz
One Small Step Can Change Your Life by Robert Maurer
The Compound Effect by Darren Hardy

APPENDIX B
Money Opportunity Log

On the next page is your monthly Money Opportunity Log. Make copies for each month, write your name at the top of each page, and then log the amount of money you created for yourself that month from each of the 12 Money Opportunities. Good luck!

To print your monthly copies of this page go to
www.CreatingFinancialLiteracyLLC.com

_____'s

Money Opportunity Log

	Money Opportunity	Amount Put Into Your Pocket
1.	Home Telephone Bill	
2.	Cell Phone Bill	
3.	Lunch and Snacks at Work	
4.	Utility Bills	
5.	Carpools and Errands	
6.	Increasing Credit Scores	
7.	Adjust Tax Withholdings	
8.	Cable/Pay Television	
9.	Personal Care, Insurance, and Banking	
10.	Luxuries and Liabilities	
11.	The Power of Lists	
12.	Money Logging	
	Monthly Money Created to Put in Your Pocket:	

Congratulations on your money creation success! Now make
sure you put all of your money to great use every month!

About the Author

Jennifer S. Matthews is a sought after motivational speaker who is known for her practical approach for helping people "get it" when it comes to understanding and managing money. She is trained as a financial coach and speaks to numerous corporations, conventions, and community organizations.

Jennifer earned master's degrees from both LaSalle University and The Johns Hopkins University. She holds Certificates of Professional Recognition in Homebuyer Education Training and Beginning to Intermediate Foreclosure Prevention, both from NeighborWorks America. She was a Delegate at the Global Summit on Financial Literacy, and participated in the White House Office of Faith Based and Community Initiatives Compass in Action Roundtable on Financial Literacy.

Jennifer was a regular guest financial expert on a consumer television show in Washington, DC for several years, and was a featured expert in a mini-documentary that aired on public television. She has also been quoted and featured in several publications. Under her leadership, the Economic Development Committee of her local chapter of Delta Sigma Theta Sorority, Inc. earned top regional and international awards for programs and community offerings. *Visit Jennifer online at: www.jenniferSmatthews.com and subscribe to her free newsletter.*